God's Livestock Policy

Stan Apps

with an Introduction by
Michael Magee

TRENCHART: Parapet Series

ƒ

LES FIGUES PRESS
Los Angeles

Designed and edited by Les Figues Press.
Printed in Canada.
Printed on Recycled Paper.

TrenchArt: Parapet
FIRST EDITION

ISBN 10:   1-934254-05-3
ISBN 13:   978-1-934254-05-9
Library of Congress Control Number: 2007941435

Les Figues Press thanks its members for their support and readership.
Les Figues Press is a 501(c)3 organization. Donations are tax-
deductible.

God's Livestock Policy is underwritten by Victor Apps. Thank you.

Les Figues would like to acknowledge the following individuals
for their generosity: Johanna Blakley, Diane & Chris Calkins,
Terry Castle, Coco Owen, Stanley Sheinbaum, and Mary & Jim
Swanson.

Publisher's Note: Special thanks to Danielle Adair, Jennifer
Calkins, Janice Lee, Susan McCabe, Vanessa Place, Maude Place,
Fergus Place, and Pam Ore.

Distributed by SPD / Small Press Distribution
1341 Seventh Street
Berkeley, CA 94710
www.spdbooks.org

TrenchArt 3/2
Book 4 of 5 in the TRENCHART Parapet Series.

ℒ

LES FIGUES PRESS
Post Office Box 7736
Los Angeles, CA 90007
323.734.4732 / info@lesfigues.com
www.lesfigues.com

This book is for

Mark Hoover,

Russell Reed,

and Amo

Poems included here have previously appeared in *Greetings* and the Ugly Duckling Presse chapbook *soft hands*.

Contents

Introduction

"Added to the natural good qualities of Mr. Covey, he was a professor of religion—a pious soul—a member and a class-leader in the Methodist church. All of this added weight to his reputation as a 'nigger-breaker.'" That's Frederick Douglass. In the context of antebellum American culture, Douglass, like Ralph Waldo Emerson, viewed such descriptions not as a problem with God, but with language.

"No forms," Emerson told an audience of fellow abolitionists in response to the Fugitive Slave Law, "neither constitutions, nor laws, nor covenants, nor churches nor bibles, are of any use in themselves. The devil nestles comfortably into them all." In his journal he privately confided that Christianity was "a religion of dead dogs." "Of course they quote the bible, & Christ & Paul, to defend slavery...these are dead forms that will cover anything."

What does Stan Apps think? "The angry book in the corner, called the / Book," he writes in these pages, " waits / like a sponge / to accept and adapt to / whatever people have been taught it says." But whether we can separate God's work from the Devil's—and what the consequences would be if we could—is a more complicated affair and, really, not the one Apps has thrown himself into in *God's Livestock Policy*.

Apps's approach to God in this book is reminiscent, in its tone, to that of Jonathan Miller's famous quip about the term "atheism," that one doesn't need it, any more than one needs a name for not believing in the tooth fairy. Apps, in a sort of postmodern turn to end all turns, simply presumes the opposite—that of course God exists—with equal cool, and then proceeds to delineate Him. Does Apps "Believe" in "God"? How the hell should I know? And who cares? What would it mean if he did? Or didn't? Apps seems to table the ontological question for a much more interesting, useful and emotionally and politically disturbing one: Given the fact that God exists, who is He? What is He like, what's His plan and who's His boss?

Apps's approach leads to some characterizations and insight both believable and incredible.

> God is bored. God loves the blank stare of the victim whose recovery is eternally delayed by further violence. He created the world so He could have this person to be near Him without contradicting Him. If all that one expects is to be hurt, then one stops expecting, so abused children actually are Nirvana.

Is this satire? Are we being asked to do something after reading it? I thought, on a first reading, of the American cultural tradition exemplified by Faulkner's character McEachern for whom "bigotry and clairvoyance were practically one" and whose "cold and implacable and undeviating conviction of both omnipotence and clairvoyance" is transferred to his stepson Joe Christmas such that "the boy's body might have been wood or stone; a post or a tower upon which the sentient part of him mused like a hermit, contemplative and remote with ecstasy and selfcrucifixion." Then I thought of Lucas Moodysson's basketball-playing abused-adolescent angels in "Lilya 4ever." As with this image, there is a kind of banality to Apps's imagery that does not detract from (and perhaps even heightens) their tragic quality. Describing razor wire, common to our prisons, our borders and our black holes of extraordinary rendition, Apps writes, "You try to climb the wire, / You cut yourself to pieces, become a / Man made of very, very deep shaving cuts." This is death late-capitalist-style; death by Gillette; death as new product. The Foucauldian implication (you did it to *yourself* by trying to climb that wall) is a killer. As are the puns on "become a man" and "man made."

There are moments in *God's Livestock Policy* where Apps tips his hand, in the form of scorching irony ("God arrives as an army-recruiter") or poignant exasperation ("Jimmy Carter, even Jimmy Carter is a murderer"). There are a series of poems toward the end of this book which seem to me in the tradition of Blake's *Songs of Experience* and/or Swift's "Description of a City Shower" (good religious men, both—look too for the allusion to Wordsworth's "We Are Seven" as a possibly fiery point of resistance to the notion that "We all must board the / Charity balloon / Into polite oblivion"). And there are moments of black humor with real social teeth (the poem "Psychedelic Snapback" may be the closest we ever get to being an internal witness to George W. Bush's actual dreams). The young Stan Apps would seem to appear in several autobiographical poems early in the text. The question, though, of whether Apps himself is one of the good guys, is not, to my mind, one of the central questions raised by this text. Personal psychology as it happens here is staged like in comic books: "This was before sorrow settled like a black butterfly between my eyes, much like the little raccoon mask that Robin the Boy-Wonder wore." It's not that this is insincere. Rather, Apps places testimony in the service of—and at the mercy of—the Good Book.

Who is God and what is He for? At one point, in the amazing myth "God's Pocket Lint," God wails, "Why did I create this thing?" Is there any hope for that world, the one that would appear to be ours? Ultimately, the temperament of *God's Livestock Policy* is most reminiscent of the darling and devastating temperament of Kafka. I'm thinking of Walter Benjamin quoting Max Brod quoting Kafka as saying, "We are nihilistic thoughts, suicidal thoughts that come into God's head." This, Kafka explained to Brod, was more casual and banal than the Gnostic view of humanity. "Our world is only a bad mood of God, a bad day of his." "Then there is hope outside this manifestation of the world that we know," Brod posited. "Oh, plenty of hope," Kafka assured him, "an infinite amount of hope—but not for us."

If the world is "a Bible made of landmines; you read it with your feet" then "a phony Bible is the greatest thing a man can offer the world." Stan Apps has done it.

Michael Magee

Cumberland, Rhode Island, 2007

God's Livestock Policy

This Book

For many years, human beings have been trying to understand the powerful being who controls the universe. He or It has been imagined many ways: as a ferocious father, slapping down his children's enemies, holding them in the corner, stunning them with roars. As a chiding ethicist repeatedly and drearily insisting on the same self-righteous tenets: do not steal, do not kill, do not rape, do not ignore the suffering of people on the street. As a friend, a counselor, a super-ego, a substitute for a missing sense of self-control, a more powerful Self (a Self in love with my itty-bitty self. I may not know the President or even any Congresspeople, but I am friends with the ruler of the Universe!) As a womanish man who sheds plump homemade tears as nourishing as chicken soup when faced with news of new atrocities. These are all reasonable descriptions, and explain many things that need to be explained, such as why some towns should be policed by armed men from far away who'll shoot anyone dumb enough to leave the house for groceries, or such as why there is starvation, why there are droughts, how earthquakes choose which town to take apart, or such as why am I so rich, why am I so special, why am I so central, or such as why are there places, why have an idea like "space," why should one thing be "distant" from another, why can't we all be simultaneous?

This book makes no attempt to explain or make sense of anything except the Almighty. Other, more difficult subjects have been left for the consideration of better men. It is naturally insipid people such as myself and all the spiritually and materially impoverished dull-thoughted human crud who live on rural routes or in the slums—we are the ones who need and love God. The wise, the witty, the admired, have resources of their own. We, so weak in perspicacity, must draw from the general resource—God, a common property like oxygen and water. Like all other common properties, corporations throw their waste in it. God is filled like a landfill with sentimental mass-produced sludge of sticky-fake emotion more revolting than your cousin Joe's used condom. But at least he wore a condom! At least something was said about God, however much it contaminated Him.

You can't take the burned-up gasoline out of the oxygen. You can't take human falsehood out of God. It has been put in, you breathe the air, you're breathing someone's soot, you think of God, you're thinking someone's self-indulgent fantasy. Jesus loves me like I love my puppy. Jesus dress me in a little costume and I'll dance, just like I dress up puppy and I hold his hands and he walks around on his little two back-feet. When you think of God, your head fills up with the stickiest most human love-notes and ambitions to kill people and build things on their land. That's OK, our almighty has it in Him and can handle it. In His vastness, infinite space exists, in which the hot air of human exhaust can diffuse and diffuse and diffuse, the particles of what we are spreading out until each of our thoughts has a million miles between them, God is that perpetually elongating pause, a territory too big to occupy. In this territory I now stake some posts and begin unrolling barb-wire and nailing signs to the posts that say "No Admittance." I have enclosed myself in an armed fortress that is God and Mine, and my love-struck gently-bleeding followers will rat-a-tat your whack-ass if you so much as steal a glance at Me, I mean He. Nevertheless, welcome. This book is for you, for your edification and understanding, I intend it to be a transformative event in your short life. I intend to reveal my secrets to you, eventually. Nothing is worthwhile that is overly easy of access. God is a Democracy, and like any Democracy, is ruled by mysterious elites. I saw the Pope whispering with that young man; is that young man conspiring to change the meaning of the Virgin Mary? He is a handsome young man, that man is. Although such things are lost on the current Pope. Someday God will let us have a little *refinement* again, my friend. Welcome, dear readers, to the finer points of the charisma.

I Have Been Enthusiasm

I have been enthusiasm, often. Believe me, I have been
     believe. I want to be approved of, which of course
     requires a form. The words in the poem. You step
     between them and they praise your wishes. With a
     whim, you can deceive yourself, and wash the ugliness
     out of the poem.
The gadgets in the poem are attackable, like her mouth
     becomes real tense. Wind blows the expression
     off of someone's face. And if what we want to do is
     couples' calisthenics at our wedding, with personal
     trainers to assist us, then the question is which gym
     will we call. I need to be encouraged correctly. Yes,
     I'm sure I will need to be tugged at, tweaked, and
     prodded—but I also want to be rewarded, with
     stage-whispers of approval—
such as a mother spills, when there are no more dishes
     in the ocean. Good men have gotten sick sometimes
     of committing violent crimes, for the better future
     that the war-profiteers have advertised—These
     men should remember that God approves of
     everything, sooner or later, and better yet the girls
     that were requisitioned will soon be arriving on a
     truck, as soon as some more locals have "volunteered"
     to trade their sex for room and
board. "Bored" is a word that expresses why things
     happen. If no one spoke, read, or wrote, or took
     off their underwear expecting admiration or a
     blank stare, then we would all be "bored." God is
     bored. God loves the blank stare of the victim
     whose recovery is eternally delayed by further
     violence. He created the world so He could have
     this person to be near him without contradicting
     him. If all that one expects is to be hurt, then one
     stops
expecting, so abused children actually are Nirvana.
     Religions without bloodstains make no sense. To

make sense, a religion must accept war as the natural lopsidedness, that disintegrates the moral fiber of those whose lifestyles consider themselves blessed. In my constitutionally-protected abuse of privacy. Wash wishes off. Following a whim that seems rather stupid is one way to feel relatively free. I am glad this writing has no destiny

to commit. I refuse to believe that any of these whims have been predestined! I admit I have been wanting to say these things, but I can no longer be bound by that. Our values thrived during the gunplay brought on by the food shortage. Our dead became new chapters in the textbook of Mechanical Defeat. Teeth fall out without a dentist. Each of our dead is a new tooth in the snapped-shut jaw of God. Dead bodies are predestined, so

the meaning of each death is the only obstacle to a history that adds up to a Heaven we commute to, through internal processes. Exaltation. Joy. We can be persuaded to experience truly wonderful transformations, which through loyalty, we prove we did deserve those Heavens where we've been.

Psychedelic Snapback

If I had wings growing out of the top of my head,
and they fluttered when I had a thought,
that would be cool,

and if when they fluttered I lifted slightly off the ground
and if at the same time a joyous rush of excitement
made of purest dopamine and serotonin in ideal angelic
mixture rushed through my head
so that my eyelids tingled and little bells in my ear-drums
tinkled and my tongue became prehensile and wrapped
itself around nearby surfaces like a licorice band-aid that
restored the world by rubbing objects full of utility and
aesthetic values so they glimmered as if newly sea-born,
and a sense of cartoon-like tragedy was then overcome
by cathartic triumph in the form of a surge of good
destruction splitting the house of my enemies in half like
the eggshell it always was, then

then

solipsism would win,
I would live alone
with the various creatures that reflect my
sense of my own majesty, in a majestic

no

in a sense of my own powerless wretched inability to
properly experience myself,
the source of this inability being the fact that I
do not exist in any form approximating
the way I have been conditioned to imagine myself.

People imagine the almighty
because they themselves wish to be everything
and everywhere at once.
The almighty wants to kill their enemies because
the almighty is only an extension of their imagined
sovereignty. They, the people,
want to fill the world with themselves, impersonally,
keeping their eccentricities out of God.

God is Love. God wants War. Love wants War. The
largest mega-church of Mom agreeing. Wearing
swimsuits near the pool. God is Swimsuit. God
wants Wearing. Swimsuit wants Love Wearing.
God is Grampa. God wants Pool. Gramps wants
Pool retiring. Mom wants Grampa to relax, mind
his condition. Skin wants Elasticity. The largest
mega-church of Swimsuit Wearing. People come
for Swimsuit Wearing. Stay for Eating Baked Goods.
Go for Sacred Image. God is Sacred Image. Do not
depict Swimsuits. Can't you Enjoy anything without
Copying it? Gramps wants Pool in shape of ring on
Pinkie-finger, shape of diamonds, shape of a
Mountain of complaints falls into poolside in the
shape of Grandma wearing a stern apron. Wearing
the stains from baking Baked Goods. God is stains
from baking Baked Goods worn around on apron.
The stern white apron with no image. Accidental
Image. Stains from Baking Baked Goods want
bleaching. God wants bleaching. Stern imageless
apron. Largest mega-church of faceless apron. Love
is Swimsuit wearing. Love is faceless apron. Love is
Baking Baked Goods. Come for the stern Love
flesh in
Pool Retiring. Stay to be congratulated on staying. Girls
and Grandmas, natural enemies. Where is the
Love? The largest mega-church in shape of ring on
Pinkie-finger, there's the Pastor, what is Love, Mr.
Pastor? God is Love. God wants War. Love wants
War. Love is Jealous. God is Angry. God is Jealous.
God is Jealous of the Love expressed by Them
idolaters. God is Jealous of the Love expressed by
them Houses, for them Realtors. God is Jealous
of the usefulness and convertibility of Real-Estate,
becoming Capital. It can hold a coach, a leather
couch. It can hold a rest, a nap. Grandpa must

Relax in his condition. God is jealous of the duality
     of Real-Estate, both body (Love a chair for comfort)
     also Spiritual (Clouds of Money Migrate along
     spirit-winds like Digitalized Geese. God is
     Digitalized Grampa Geese. God is faceless apron
     Gramma Baked Goods, God wants bleaching, God
     wants war, God wants Poolside Service Swimsuit
     apron Baking War on Pinkie-finger Shape of
     Diamonds. Jealous them Idolators, Swimsuit war
     commanding flesh-kill Pool Retiring, all die Suburb,
     Grampa, Gramma, natural enemies, because they
     love the same thing, love the same God, love
Themselves equally, hate each other to love themselves,
     Love the Same, ONE GOD Grampagramma

It was America, so God would come
in the form
of a labor-
saving device.

The car won't start and neither will the goat:
even God practices planned obsolescence.
The car won't start and neither will the goat,
and now the goat

has to shrink, to fit inside
a brain. And someday even
the idea of the goat
won't start.

We shoveled so much shit to make that
orchard blossom, and when it blossomed
it was ours and it was God's:
it was our gift to God and His to us.

Around that time I invented my God,
a shy guy observing his Creation nervously,
anticipating Man's left hook, Man's sudden
sky-denying uppercut.

My God rode upon my Mom's God's shoulders
to get a little extra distance from the Earth.
My God could never see the point of effort—
since anything could just spring up at any

moment from the vast Void of his Thought,
a cloudy afternoon
when a beam of light
without a retinue

or trumpet or agenda or
twelve-year-old angel of unblemished skin or
white of robes
or consequence

rains bright small specks of thereness
through my mind, like being listened to
by open bits of light inside my head,
tiny glowing open ears of pure light-headedness

that close
and then
I'm listening to my
self

just as
lovingly as God had,
but it means less
and I mean less.

COMPETITION

When I'm in college, my mother takes up the religious
manifesto pretty much full time. The fanatic pep with
which she produces these documents is a nagging mirror
of my own ambitions. Borrowing my typewriter, she
quickly pecks the e-key out of use, and soon reverts
to handwriting, in big block letters that will xerox
clearly. The resulting documents are ugly, but Mom is no
aesthetician. She is a saint.

Meanwhile, I am taking my chemistry notes in
iambic pentameter, which almost causes me to fail.
My poems always mention blue. Blue animals, blue
Christ, blue bruise on the inside of a thigh. I describe
masturbation in terms of a visitation by space aliens.
The aliens are blue, with damp fur like moss. They speak
in italics, making small-talk about fish. . .

Mom's advantage is, she throws nothing away All
she writes has God in it, redeeming. I have a garbage
bag full of paper, of words almost demolished by others
written over them, my own brain's contribution to
the dump. In my brain is a very little god, reaching
my writing hand in tiny stutters. This god only thinks
coherently once or twice a day. Mom's god is a
downpour. He has hoarded a hundred secrets, just for
her, in one verse from the Book of Revelation. These
secrets are those of a specialist, and require a specialist's
language. The lion of the unpronounceable, the dove of
blah-blah, blah. People see her writings at my apartment,
and I hurriedly reassure them. Personally I have nothing
against the Pope.

I write a poem in which Mom dies, is buried, and a
tree sprouts from her grave. The fruits of the tree are

xeroxed, hand-stapled pamphlets that contain a truth
so profound that God Himself blinks his one eye at it in
amazement, and the void where he lives is redesigned
into a mathematical mesh of prophecies, frowning like an
armed alarm clock, like an indictment of good times. No
one knows exactly what to say about it. The aliens had
more social relevance, and I feel that if I explain, I'll be
a jerk... So I put it in my garbage bag, which by now is
the same size I am, dense with old euphoria, heavy as a
prolapsed soul.

She lived in a broken car, alone.

The protestant embarks, upon
what is revealed
which is always
something he had known but not quite known,

embarks
in armored arks
upon the rushing waters of
the world flowing full of contradictions.

She lived in a broken car, alone.
Sunbeams reach to any place we dream of.

Strong knowledge, like a lock-box,
is where the protestant
keeps God. It is the same
as any form of wealth,

the nature of a good thing is
we guard it. God
is our treasure
and we protect him well.

She lived in a broken car, alone.
Sunbeams paint the dust-motes almost-colors.

God replicates for each of us,
teaches how right and wrong
are versions of his manuscripts
to be rewritten as we go along.

Our replicas of God are kept
inside our head,
because our God is an idea
not a tiger or a pig.

She lived in a broken car, alone.

The clouds are thinking
lonely thoughts, so unaware,
so full of air so unaware
that it is air.

God is like an antidote
to roleplay desperation
when the shapeless heart
can't justify a wardrobe.

I will wear the heavy tablets
in my hands
so they'll be stiff
and good to thwack you with.

She lived in a broken car, alone.

Some pleasant people
like to run away.
They do not like to do
what you believe their duty is.

For those pleasant people, God
is always farther on,
but the most they ever learn about him
is his further beckoning.

She lived in a broken car, alone.

Some thoughts are almost self-sufficient,
some ideas have their own self-interests,
that are not changeable and brief,
that are not changeable and brief like men and women,

The safest place in this world, the warmest place,
is to be inside one of those thoughts,
to be among the ranks of the facilitating class,
the managers, the spokesmodels, the priests,

giving an eternal thought a push
into the new eternities appearing in new minds.

I have some goals, they are somewhere near me.
I will do justice to some of them
some time. They will enable me to find
a future, and I will do something there.

It will all involve a lot of repetition.
Things that happen only once have barely any meaning.
Things that happen only once can barely be enjoyed,
when you have not learned how to enjoy them yet.

She lived in a broken car, alone.
Sunbeams rush to any place we dream up.

Coyotes have short digestive tracts
so they can eat things that are rotten
and pass them through themselves so quick
that they will not get sick.

So it is in love, you need not
take the trouble to find worthwhile persons:
it does not matter who they are, provided
that the time you take with them is brief.

She lived in a broken car, alone.
I was born in the passenger-seat,
and I have held on to it,
outlasting many drivers, many drives.

Everywhere Melissa went, she felt
a feeling following backing her up:
that she would be OK, because
she was still learning

and the soul's immune, while it is in school,
and the body, good child of the soul,
the soul feeding spoonfuls of encourage
to the body, hurry now.

She lived in a broken car, alone.

The saint was tired of the holy text,
so sick and tired of reciting it,
so he added some flourishes of his own,
of his own personality to it

in the corners where,
like gargoyles, they stared out
from the otherwise
perfected good.

God's opinion must be distinguished from
his Law.
He might change his opinion
but he will not change his Law.

He might grow a new body
here on Earth, like an opinion
that it is worthwhile to visit here on Earth
and say some things, and disappear.

I.

I was born on January 29th, 1974 in Toronto General
Hospital. I was about to be circumcised when my
mother yelled out that I not be cut: "He's suffered
enough," she said, or something like that. This is hearsay;
I can't remember. It's going to be positively pages before
I tell you anything that I remember. Life is like that; it
starts with people telling you what it was like when it
happened to them. Luckily, they lie, in order to conceal
from you how evil the existence is to which you have
been admitted. Their act of concealing reality from you
is the first act of creating Heaven, which already exists
after the world, out where everyone is dead, and maybe
someday can be convinced or lured or lied to, in order
to convince it to come lie down here, where we are,
like a bear-rug beneath our most plastic playmate, like a
thirty-pound statue of a dollar-bill hung around the neck
of our most bearded gigolo.

II.

"He's suffered enough," or something like that, she said: Thereby establishing, right from the get-go, her role as an indulgent parent, provider of the sixteen-million comic books that flutter round my neurons recombinatorially. The Cold War had, from a strategic standpoint, already been won when I was born, with Reagan yet to come, a form of crystalline leather encrusted with strategic Christ, a strategic Christ dressed up in astrological fairy-dust that colored the open veins a hummingbird-happy silver. Nixon and Kissinger had, by equipping antiCommunist (anyone who already had money was automatically "antiCommunist") regimes with weapons, many weapons, multitudes of weapons, weapons being used, "Cold War" (?), lots of dead bodies, you would have noticed it if it were in your neighborhood, probably. Muscular slaughter of communist intellectuals whose confused ideals would have led them to slaughter millions in an angst-ridden effeminate way. Meant that peace was about to hit like a middle-class tax hike. No, silly, it meant peace was about to hit like **prosperity**, a thing absolutely to be avoided, because here in the war-universe, scarcity is power, a Wall around a scarcity is power.

III.

Next memory: a photographer took my picture. He
may have actually been Satan, or a child-molester. No
problem; I was never unsupervised except when I ran
nude around the block or leapt up and down with boots
on on a glass table. Anyway, the pictures were pretty.
I will never look so pretty again. Some people use it
up quickly. This was before sorrow settled like a black
butterfly between my eyes, much like the little raccoon
mask that Robin the Boy-Wonder wore.

IV.

Strange anxious yellow fumes of a fumigator who
fumigated himself in order to be clean. Chemicals, which
are contained in everything, are often poisonous. In
an urban setting, many door-handles are touched by
a distressingly large number of people. Large parties
are fun. Anybody can become a family. You have the
freedom to create relationships of all kinds. Use of
drugs creates a greater social fluidity which enables
connections and mergers and deals that you would not
expect to last for a long time on the outside.

V.

The map is like a list of little doorways, little rabbit-
holes into which you could fall. Creative misreading of
a map about wind currents creates the impression that
a certain section of the map is safe from wind-borne
contaminants. Don't tell the border patrol about the
filled-in-blanks releasing flavorful air-borne molecules.
Nixon was gone; it was safe to return to America: it was
like the Big Bad Witch was dead. No one that mean, in
terms of open expressions of aggressive postures, would
be elected again until the second George Bush. It was a
beautiful 27 years of wimpy non-threatening Presidents
who acted like they knew that massive groups of people
hated them. And of course Reagan who acted like he
knew that massive groups of people loved him, which
he corresponded to by acting loveable and keeping
his aggressions down to mere verbal warnings of the
Armageddon which his full wrath might unleash, much
like Yahweh would have done.

VI.

Toronto, by the way, is beautiful. There are trees in the
park and sometimes when you walk on a path between
the trees with your mother, a gold light surrounds you
which is so perfect it is also silver. Everything that
is fully-gleaming looks the same. You can only make
distinctions by being morose. Waco has these trees that
look like they've been aged by being dipped in cobwebs
until their skin contains the sprouting eggs of cobwebs.
You live in a house with a driveway that leads to a road
and the road goes to other houses that are a mile
or more away. There is no way to walk between the
houses unless you walk along the road, in which case the
cars go by unpleasantly fast right next to you; you stand
in a ditch below them while they pass. Waco is named
after the Huaco Indians: they left a lot of arrowheads,
apparently because they went through a lot of them, the
way a chain-smoker goes through matches (lighters had
not been invented in the time of the Huaco Indians).

VII.

I've already told you one thing I remember, about the
cars going by you in the ditch, so obviously I over-
estimated how much I knew before falling back on my
own experience. The problem, philosophically, with
falling back on your own experience is that you don't
know how representative your experience is. There
may be only one person who ever had an experience
like yours, and of course he'll be your brother, or she'll
be your sister, but you won't be able to found a country,
the two of you. You will be able to found a conversation,
which is more beautiful than a public presence, because
it is so much larger than memory, and certain things
have been repeated in it more than even the most-
overplayed song, the song that you overplayed, to give
you something you could barely listen to. Listening
to my own beliefs like a man in a city listens to traffic:
barely noticing. And a blue man floats above the
storytelling, like my own blue eye, like the Human Torch,
except composed of some sort of God-Magnet Celestial
Cool-Blue Relaxation Secret Waves. Imaginative waves
remove the sting from when the dragonfly of World
Z pushed his stinger through the membrane into our
world, and abandoned it, and now World Z is an inept
nowhere without the wherewithal to ever reach us
again, to ever reclaim the injury done to us when it
pushed information through our blue.

Sunlight marries the sun
Before leaving
With a come-hither shrug,
Blown away by some sort of cosmic

Need to expurge.
Moonlight dances
Around the moon,
Without making promises.

Sunlight barrels down
Into the Earth
And hurts it, until it gets covered by
Surface infections (us)

(and them) (and the beautiful socially-maladjusted
Plants). These plants are so good but they want to
Die. They soak up solar energy then
Die. And then we eat them or burn them or

Build shelving units. This is done with the
Sunlight they contain. Who would have thought you
Could build a shelving unit out of sunshine but
It just takes time. Sunlight becomes the

Ability to live, whereas the sun
Is a Source Too Rich to be Nourished-By,
Too much beneficial stuff Erases because
Its Claim is so great that it makes you disappear in Full.

GOD'S POCKET LINT

God reached down in his pocket and pulled out a.
What is it? It's a wad of pocket lint. White lint with
a greasy texture from those moments when God's
unclean fingers absently adjust the nubbly bottoms of
his pockets. The wad God found in his pocket actually
was the location where he'd put Heaven. God lost
Heaven one day, because he had so many things in his
pockets, so much to organize. It doesn't matter if God
loses Heaven because Heaven is self-sustaining and
self-organizing. Lost Heaven found itself touching down
softly in a lint-wad. Heaven's sheep-white cottoniness is
not infiltrated by the greasy grayish white of the lint-puff
tucked around it. Who tucked Heaven into this friendly
lint-puff? God's split personality, the Devil! Sometimes
God thinks he is someone else; this someone else is a
slippery individual called the Devil! If you haven't heard
about him, he's bad news! His naughtiness is legendary.
It's rumored he may have sold nuclear centrifuges to
Iran! It was when God was being this someone else, this
Devil, this individual, that he put Heaven into the wad of
pocket-lint and tucked heaven in quite deep so none of
its golden palaces or shiny streets were visible. All that
is visible is the white lint with a greasy texture because
God never bothers to wash His hands because He is
immune to germs and fear of germs is why you wash
your hands so God never bothers to wash His hands so
stuff like grease and oily fluids and trace amounts and
bits of dust and bits of hair from cats and flakes of skin
from humans whose flaky hands he held, to comfort
them and to protect. God's memory is on his hands in
the forms of trace amounts of all bodies and all souls,

all of which he's handled. God is a wonderful patriarch who never has sexual thoughts about anyone, not even girls! His split-personality, the Devil, on the other hand, is a lascivious, lecherous, licentious, legalistic, libelous, laminated report-cover and the report he hands to Teacher in its sleek plastic cover is a complete report of Wrong-doing, Human Suffering, Contamination, Filth, Condemnation, Murderous Violence, Thoughtless Killing of Africans, Thoughtful Killing of Arabs, Premeditated Gradual Cancerous Collapse of Chinese Industrial Peasants in Slave-Labor Shoesize Factories. Oh, he's so bad, that Devil! Oh! Oh! Oh! And why did he hide Heaven? And does God know where it is? Did God reach down in his pocket for a reason just then or was God just absently moving his conceptual arm and hand and placing them into his conceptual pocket because he was looking for a Concept, but all he found was a bitty-itty wad o' lint? God's bitty-itty wadolint. What's God going to do with it? Is he going to blow on it, like a boy blows on a dandelion, so the greasy grayish white will fall away from the pure-white, sheep-white, golden palaces and shiny streets? It doesn't matter if He finds Heaven because Heaven is self-sustaining and self-organizing. It needs no leadership. It does not resemble a business. Some do not get more for doing less while others who get less do more. O no. Some do not get more for doing the same amount while others get less for doing the same amount. O no. Some do not get the same amount while doing less while others get the same amount while doing more. O no. It needs no leadership. There are no opportunities for leadership. The strict Chinese bureaucracy of Heaven denounces leadership with a collective "Hear! Hear! Hear!" and God imposes no force from outside, because He doesn't have to, naturally. He chose to set Heaven up that way, because he set Earth up differently, and Earth requires him to constantly make adjustments and fiddle with and labor over it and add rubber bands to hold bits together that used to fit together but have come apart and become weaponized towards each other. Earth just wants to exchange war with itself and it drives God nutty. "Why did I create this terrible thing?" God wails. And to comfort himself, absently wiggles his pocket-lint. And on this occasion pulls it out of His pocket, and looks at it, with an empty face... What will he ever do with it?

God's Cottage

God woke in his cottage in the alpine wilderness,
where he retired for a part of every year to build new
microbes and viruses to afflict mankind next winter.
At those times when He occupied his cottage, it was
surrounded by high walls of snow, so there was NO
chance of humans showing up to bother him. Of course,
as always, God's omniscient telepathy caused Him to
experience at every moment all the agonies and, worse
yet, the fevered rages and malicious fantasies of human
beings. But it was much worse for him up in Space
where he usually hid, because Space is a vacuum through
which telepathic info travels uninhibitedly. Within the
atmosphere, on the other hand, the noise was muted,
and muted even more by the thick curtains of pure
white life-destroying snow that settled steadily around
his cottage.

God had only 3 beings for company in the cottage,
the most visible of which was an unfinished homunculus
named Glathull, who lay in the corner sulking about how
God wouldn't get around to finishing him. Glathull was
one of those organisms which God had decided, in the
midst of working on him, simply could not be released
into the wild. It is a little-known fact that should God
complete an organism, that organism immediately comes
into existence somewhere on Earth, usually in a rain-for-
est or in the digestive tract of a hyena or in the phlegm
of a man coughing on the subway or some other espe-
cially bioactive place. God realized, just before finishing
Glathull, that if Glathull existed, he would slay all humans
with his unusually fast reflexes, superior strength, and
due to the fact that the only thing he liked to eat was

the human pineal gland. God considered going backward and leaving out some of these overly deadly traits, but that would have turned the design into something not terribly special: what's one more killer mammal, more or less? Rather than making an interesting design into something banal and average, God decided to just not finish the thing. Perhaps at a later time, if He were working on an even more violent and deadly ecosystem, Glathull could be introduced to that one. But God in his compassion half-animated Glathull in an unfinished homuncular state, to be His butler. Of course, God does not need to eat, but he does like to drink invigorating teas made from South-American stimulants from deep, deep in the jungle, many of which are either unknown to humans or are extinct due to "slash and burn" farming tactics invented by shit-for-brains leisure class white people. These teas, to be made very well, require a lot of complex boiling, infusing, grating, peeling, grinding, and various other culinary practices which Glathull, with his faster-than-human intellect and reflexes, is able to perform satisfactorily.

By the way, the part of Glathull that is missing is his stomach and intestines. Unable to eat, Glathull has to be on an IV, and constantly snorts huge amounts of cocaine to keep an imitation of vigor in his unfinished and anguished body. He also drinks huge amounts of coffee. He does have a bladder, which is constantly over-full and causes him severe back-aches.

God was also accompanied by an invisible angel named Algorithm Two. This angel operated as a server on which God stored the Laws of Physics for access by the thought-structures of successful physicists and experimental mathematicians. Unbeknownst to the intrepid thinkers trying to discover the details of the Laws and thereby fully comprehend the Universe, God had designed the Laws as a self-modifying system, that mutated unpredictably without external input. Because, of course, the Universe (or Polyverse, more properly) has no outside. The problem with such a system, of course, is how can an evolving system avoid becoming non-viable? DNA code has the life of the organism containing it to keep it honest; failed code results in failed animals and is therefore not perpetuated. If the Polyverse's rules change unpredictably, how is it that the changes never make the Polyverse break up into unrelated surds or suddenly become compacted into a super-concentrated point again? Why doesn't gravity just become less, causing all planets and stars to fall apart? Because there is a four millisecond delay in which each new set of rules is modeled within the stomach of God's third constant companion, the obese angel referred to as Complete Exception. Each new rule-set is enacted inside of Complete Exception, and if the modelverse formed inside collapses or explodes then C.E. responds to his internal indigestion by releasing a high-pitched squeal that is the "Kill Universe" signal. This signal erases Algorithm Two's short-term memory, which means that the flawed code retroactively ceases to exist, and therefore is not realized in the Polyverse. Meanwhile, Complete Exception shits the retroactively Abortedverse into the Void and then, if it was a particularly bad few milliseconds, takes a shower and a nap while Algorithm Two temporarily recycles the currently existing code. The moments when Algorithm Two is "re-running" code for a Polyverse that is that way already are those moments in the day when everything seems static, lifeless, and irrelevant; those are moments when Creation has temporarily stopped and everyone or everything throughout Creation experiences acute discomfort in the form of a sense of infinite boredom and stagnation.

The Creation continues, by stops and starts, and each new incarnation and addition is the source of all pleasure, satisfaction, or joy experienced anywhere in the Polyverse. God set it up that way because, being the Creator, he values Creation above all other things.

Suddenly a new virus comes into existence on God's work-table, where he has been playing with some colds and flus, hybridizing them. Instantly, some children in a hospital in Estonia begin to die. Their immune systems are not effective enough against this virus in combination with a more typical flu that they also have. This virus only affects a few people, and then becomes extinct; it was not contagious enough to escape the hospital. God only promises each new creation one chance. A created being has to come out of its Mommy (or asexual progenitor, or invaded host) ready to grab on and smear or inject its DNA (or other code) as deeply and/or broadly in the Polyverse as possible...

Glathull grunts jealously in a corner, washing out the inside of the hollow log in which God likes one of His herbs brewed. If only someday he could exist... He would show the stupid humans. He would fill every yard of his intestines with a river of warm pineal juice...

FOR EXAMPLE

We are all just imitations of exemplary lives,
such as those of Jesus or Abe Lincoln
or someone who was a good father
or Jack the Ripper or Hagar
or Noah keep the children in an ark
or serenity like an invasion of
charmed quarks into strange butter
or Leopold Senghor or Napoleon Dynamite
or Captain America or Captain Marvel
or Collected Poems of or Warhol
or Kentucky Fried Chicken's
or the Arch-Angel of the Half-Nelson
or Walt Whitman or Joseph Stalin
or Al Capone or Scarface or
the Notorious B.I.G. or B.I.G. M.O.N.E.Y.
or B.I.B. or Marilyn Monroe
or Emma Goldman or Cindy Sherman
or John Lennon saying
no one's going to dig you if you dig Chairman Mao
or hail Elvis or Little Richard
or Beethoven or Claude Debussy
or a balloon with a flaming human face,
radiant in an infinite way.

Almost everyday
I imagine what it would be like
to be a deeply moral person
who shoots people.

I would shoot wrong ideas
so that the whole world,
the one world, the heaven,
would cry and feel better.

I would wear huge head garments
with huge pictures of human
suffering on them,
attacking censorship.

In my imagination, I would punch
all the bad people over and
over again, so they wouldn't dare
punch anyone again.

In the silence when
I monopolize all punches
almost everyday
I enjoy morality.

The world betrays my feelings
as the bad people
hurt me over and over
through the innocent, my proxies.

Censorship cannot stop
this poignant flow of blood;
we can only shape the flow
like a river, to irrigate morals.

We are, many of us, improvisations
or imitations,
conceited
reenactments of

the life of
an average
hero, such as
Jesus, an everyday guy with a wild

imagination,
who persevered
in the face of a stone
rolled over his grave, which he looked

out from, like
a face in the wine-stain on
a napkin, except that it
went through rocks, and the blood was pure light

tinted red by being in a lava-lamp.
Or, alternatively
our heroes are heroic soldiers
who dedicate their lives to

the idea of weapons,
which is
to kill, in the true
anger of the wounded son, as if Jesus, in this view, were

the sort of frustrated
kid for whom it's easier
to be told what to do by some muscular
son-of-a-gun, rather than

read books (the angry book in the corner, called the
Book, waits,
like a sponge
to accept and adapt to
whatever people have been taught it says).

He had been trying to be an example of how to live, but then he died, and against his will became an example of how to die. This was particularly important in those days, when they all died very young.

In many countries now they still die very young, just like they used to, but here we have adopted new models of how to die, involving persons who are so old that they barely respond to stimuli, in antiseptic rooms with tubes of fluids flowing into them, refreshing and invigorating them enough that they can blink. If you're going to die, you might as well wait until most of you has faded away already. Losing everything at once is monstrous; losing in dribs and drabs is more manageable. It's like slowly falling out of love with life, slowly getting divorced from one's own metabolism, slowly losing track of one's convictions, slowly saying goodbye to one's soul as it turns its face slowly away and casts its gaze out far, into the half-lit yawning space of God.

Martyrs are for suckers; for the ones who die young. In some countries, almost everyone dies of the struggle, but the winners of the struggle come here and wait for it in furnished rooms near hospitals, ignoring the armies of martyrs, forgetting the fiery songs, admiring how thin the skin is as it gets closer and closer to the bone. "My compliments on how long you have lived sir," the old man says to the mirror. "These days I barely recognize you my old friend," the old man says to the mirror. "Your enemies still look the same, in their pictures on the posters and the pamphlets and the banners, but you have displayed an ingenious ability to adapt." Finally the old man forgets why he had to survive so much, why he had wanted to fight so hard, why he had been willing to kill to win. And then he's completely ready. "Who?" the old man says to the mirror.

I'm going to be everybody when I grow up,
said the boy in the bathtub
whose head was a fiery birthday cake.

I'm going to be a race-car driving scientific journalist
who runs for Congress to reform how trees are treated
and whose official address is in a tree, in a tree-house where

imaginative tea-parties allow little boy/girls
to re-enact the French Revolution with
a restful pillow and a frozen bloodstain

and my wife will grow flowers that smell like steak
and flowers that smell like the freshness inside of sleep
and she will grow bushes with buds that look like golden keys

said the boy in the bathtub,
and a small blue plastic figurine with a plastic M-16
and a small blue plastic helmet and a plastic uniform that
        won't come off

said, *Off with his head!*
And the chopped-off birthday cake fell in the tepid water,
flaming like a star, the fiery cake dropped in the tepid water.

And the mushy cake broke up into globules and briefly
        clogged the drain,
and the tub over-flowed, turning the house into a swamp,
a White Trash nightmare where no one gets educated,

but then a brand-new cake baked in the old one's place
like a blood-blister atop the sheared-off neck,
and the boy benefited from another candle.

The boy in the swamp, the boy whose whole house was
        a bathtub,

whose head was a fiery birthday cake, flaming defiantly,
swam through his bedroom and his parents' bedroom
    and his brothers' bedrooms and his sisters'
    bedrooms,

collecting mementos to be worn in a future life,
keeping his head above water for the sake of the living
    candles;
he said, *I'm going to plant a prophecy, I'm going to found a*
    plague,

I'm going to build a more painful hairbrush,
I'm going to shovel smell into the engine-room of God,
I'm going to be convinced there really is a small star in my
    forehead,

I'm going to be everybody, because I can't decide,
I'm too big to make my own decisions, only God,
whom I will also be, can make my decisions for me.

My aunt would visit me
in my Christian home
with Buddhist thoughts
when I was alone:

my Christian home was
a Christian home because
my mother was a Christian
and in fact she owned the home

My aunt meant to help me
by giving me another opportunity,
didn't I deserve
Buddha as much as Jesus?

So I had both
They both had eyes like the eyes
of a kitten died
of being put to sleep

because of cancer, because
we do not deserve to suffer
But we have to suffer but
suffering is nothing:

a giant passive force
supposedly
withstands.
My aunt suffered and my mother suffered, both

An empty bowl of milk
waits on the floor
for the people of the floor, the humble
scum, who snack on dust

would visit me
with Buddhist thoughts
when I was alone:
it was sneaky, sneaky little emptinesses

Imagine a creation ruled
by the silent and forgiving anger
of the humble, the excluded
dead, and imitations of the dead

Human beings get upset
and they want to be calm
without fear, even though
Violence surrounds them, dressed up as God, the Awful
        Imitator stained

To Oscar Romero

Property is a man from Europe. God gave America to him.
God is motionless, like Property. God waits.
Exquisite unliving objects made of Gold and sweat
Wait with God in a quiet place in Europe.

When people are not allowed to unionize, God looks at them.
When people cannot go on strike
Because they will be beaten up, God looks.
These people, worked so hard (hard work makes you virtuous),

These humble people look at God, and God looks.
They are the humble people of the floor
Lying there tired or else thrown there.
God is sympathetic to them. God knows they deserve

The exact hard life they live, worked like mules,
Because it is that hard life that makes them look to God.
Furthermore, Property needs them to work, just like that
And when they are used up, they go to Heaven and that's settled.

Remember, Property brought God with him
To this new-found land. Property gave God
All these new people to believe in, and God must know his place
In this land. God is a subordinate from Europe in this land,

2nd Banana in the Grand BananaLand!
And yet, there are men of God here who do not know God's place.
There are men of God who talk about God's Earthly Kingdom,
A world where treasure is human life, a good life (whatever
        that means).

The landowners live somewhat pleasant lives, with the comforts,
Many comforts. Their lives are pretty good, not bad,
A little sad, a little guilty, sometimes,
And there is fear, of course, that sticky fear that surrounds wealth

Just as poverty surrounds wealth. Fear sticks to the little shacks.
Men have to break into some of the shacks, to see who's there.
There can be bad thoughts in a little shack, bad men
Who would rather fight than work. Property has to kill them.

Well, they were killing the peasants at a faster than normal rate.
And Romero, he was God's man, from the Vatican
And he knew God's place, knew the sort of leash God wore
In El Salvador, a nation named for God.

But a certain friend of Romero's was killed,
And this friend was lying in a church, and next to him
A very old man was lying, dead, and a very young boy was
     lying, dead.
And Romero saw something when he saw this spectacle.

He had never been political, but suddenly he changed.
He forgot God's place. Now he thought God wanted killing
     to stop.
Who knows if someone talked to him. Satan, enemy of
     Property,
Speaking through his bushy beard of Karl Marx,

Speaking through Romero's mouth, and Romero speaking
     on behalf of God,
Speaking for the humble people of the floor, the poor.
He said that what the government was doing was not
     worth it,
He said the government must not kill anybody anymore.

God was not waiting anymore. The exquisite unliving objects
Were lonely now. God left them where they sat,
The statuettes and crucifixes, gold and gems and craftsman's
     frozen touch.
God could not be their companion anymore. God sought
     living friends.

Romero's assassin sent God back among the dead,
And the statuettes and crucifixes, gold and gems
Did not give any indication of gladness, did not give any
     welcome back to God,
Did not change, did not move, as God resumed their
     vigil with them.

Property is silent, and Property demands silence.
Everything in the world is owned. God must stay out.
Outside the world, God may say what he wants.
Keep your Heaven out, with Romero, where Property
     sent him.

Barbed wire is for cows,
Razor wire is for humans,
Humans require sharper wire
Because of they have thumbs.

Barbed wire has sharp 5-pointed barbs
Every few inches on a metal wire
That is one of 5 parallel wires
Attached to a fencepost, and another fencepost,

And another fencepost, and
It could cross the world
But if you have thumbs
You can gently pull apart two of the wires with the barbs

And slip yourself between the wires, carefully
Or, you could climb the wire
Positioning your feet between the barbs
And vault over to the other side (off the fencepost).

If you are without thumbs, and are too large to simply run
Beneath the bottom-wire, you are stuck.
Cows wait for whatever might happen
Inside a field like (The skill in designing animal pens

Was what led to creating human pens)
They don't know, because they don't, what might happen.
Razor wire, on the other hands, responds to the thumb
Problem. Useful at national borders, it consists of

Long thin very-sharp curved razors, very similar to
Over-sized straight razors, except these are curved
To follow the wire. You try to climb the wire,
You cut yourself to pieces, become a

Man made of very, very deep shaving cuts.

God lived in a cloud above a book.
Pages of the book burned, the smoke reached up to him
and changed the color of his cloud, to gray or black.

God favored livestock production,
rather than grain and vegetable production,
because God was carnivorous and His hair was full of blood.

Also God liked how the livestock were enslaved,
and how the ownership of livestock placed fences on the land,
and also gates, and barb-wire and

its cruel cousin, razor wire, to keep
certain people in certain areas
where the death-rates are higher, because tribal war

is war of attrition, war of Death the Mathematician
(we want the shortest life
for our most distant cousin) . . .

God liked how the eyes of the livestock
water in the morning, and how the livestock rolled in
the waste they had made, and wore their filth in their soft hair.

God liked how the saliva of the livestock
paused below their snouts and gleamed
as the sunlight of the morning spilled

Sun's glory like a face red as the Lord's
drops into the water-hole
where Life gathers messily exuberant

with bugs skimming and jumping,
skittering on clots of algae,
drowning, kicking out concentric circles. . .

The Devil and God

The Devil has secrets, and God has mysteries. Myster-
ies are not to be confused with secrets. A secret, as
long as it remains secret, can conceal or prevent harm;
a mystery, as long as it remains mysterious, can con-
ceal or prevent greatness. A photograph that reveals
exactly who asphyxiated toddlers is a secret. As long as
it remains a secret, harm to the toddlers is concealed.
As long as it remains a secret, harm to the stranglers is
prevented. Huge file-folders full of secrets contain great
potential to reveal and to cause harm; the Devil has
a big big bag full of folders full of secrets, which looks
a great deal like Santa Claus's bag. Sometimes these
folders are left out in the moonlight, for the fathers of
the toddlers or the goodwives of the stranglers to look
at. To asphyxiate a toddler without leaving marks is of
course an interesting skill, although rarely practiced
by professional operatives. A photograph that shows
how the face of a living man has the face of a dead man
superimposed upon the first face is a mystery. There are
many experts assigned by the powerful to explain how
the mysteries are obvious fakes. As long as it remains a
mystery, known to few believed by fewer, the greatness
of the living man is concealed. As long as it remains a
mystery, seen by none assumed untrue by everyone,
the greatness of the dead man is prevented from being
recognized within the living man. God showers us with
mysteries to help us to achieve greatness: mysterious
words and pictures and events occur reliably from time
to time within our lives. We are trained to dismiss
these as incompatible with predominating scenarios. We
live within these scenarios which conceal from us our

own greatness. Everyone of us, or most ones anyway,
is so great that God spends all his time communicat-
ing with us through miniscule signals intended to evoke
our faithful greatness, that we might therefore abandon
predominating scenarios, turn our back on the theatri-
cal rituals of humiliation and empowerment enacted by
ten-thousand human dogs, and discover God and our
own greatness both at once in a martyr-play of social
failure, when our failure to keep up with obligatory
social nonsensicals of rubbing filthy dirt on our own
faces, concealing our greatness by offering obedience
to ungreat human dogs—it catches up to us, humanity
catches up to us, we encounter our full greatness when
we are turned into homeless people, supposedly scum
pariahs, worthless losers, psychotics who won't take
our meds. But words won't take away our greatness,
because God is THE Word (I threw the rest of them
away. This is where I threw them. It is a mystery, so
merely looking at it will not necessarily mean. God gives
us true democracy, which equals: Total contempt for the
ideas of our fellow men.)

Angels and Agents

An angel is like an undercover agent; an angel tries to
seem to be a man or woman. Sometimes undercover
government agents might try to seem like angels also, as
part of their cover. Only the most beautiful government
agents can try this. Angels don't wear make-up either;
they just have a quality of vitality, a "glow of health."
Of course angels are not literally glowing; that would
make things too obvious. Angels actually do not have
gender, so they're like men without stubble, men without
testosterone-fueled rage. An angel cannot be undressed,
although lustful people will want to. Whereas God-
fearing people will have no interest in the angels other
than to feed them, have a little chat, and put a roof over
their heads. As always, God uses sexuality to weed out
the bad apples, the ones who can't control themselves.
Angels are like women but without nurturing instincts;
they are gentle, but destroying the town means nothing
to them. Angels destroy gently, a skill that government
agents admire and wish to duplicate. But the calm of a
destroying angel is based on knowing the absolute good
of the power for whom the angel works. Government
agents destroy with jittery hands because they cannot
know the moral status of the power for whom they
work. Of course, they like to assume it's pretty good;
they feel they can safely assume that the moral status
of the government is pretty good. But a government is
made out of so many minds and surely some of those
are harboring evil. Angels normally arrive at night, knock
on the door and ask for food and shelter. 8 out of 10
who are asked will tell the Angels to go away, and 3 out
of those 8 will say rude or insulting words while they

reject the angels. I out of 10 will invite the angels in for good reasons; this ten percent of the populace are the blessed. The government knows which ten percent of the populace is the blessed, and in their files they refer to this blessed tenth as the "suckers". When undercover agents pretend to be angels, they go to the homes of the blessed, and try to sucker spiritual information and financial donations out of them. They try to infiltrate and use the blessed by telling them spiritual misinformation concocted by government bureaucrats. The purpose of this misinformation is to make the blessed confused, malleable, and war-like, so they will go along with and participate in violence against resource-rich nations and non-Christian minorities. How do those bureaucrats sleep at night? They take drugs that make them fall asleep and hide their dreams from them. Spiritual information contained in dreams is a deadly threat to bureaucrats; they defend themselves against it with drugs. Dark circles around their eyes and jittery hands result. I out of 10 who are asked to shelter angels invite the angels in in hopes of seducing them. A smaller sub-section of these might even attempt to rape the angels, when they find the angels are not seduceable. The government knows which ten percent of the populace will attempt to seduce or molest angels; in their files they refer to this tenth as the "pervs." When undercover agents pretend to be angels and want easy sex, they go to the homes of the pervs, and try to sucker perverted information and financial donations out of them. There's always a day when an undercover agent pretending to be an angel wakes up and is not beautiful anymore. A grey look, dark circles around the eyes, jittery hands, and a look like steel in the eyes, as if the eyes were knives aimed toward you. These agents are given promotions and work desk-jobs as bureaucrats, figuring out which towns to destroy. The government wants to figure out which towns angels are going to destroy, and demonstrate its supremacy by destroying them first, so God will have no chance to do anything.

The Devil's Shoes

God was wearing the Devil's shoes, stepping on the
earth. Bam! Bam! Stepping on the souls of men which
crack like eggshells, releasing cruelties dressed up in
Sunday clothes of righteousness. And men and women
wear the fashionably low-key garments of cleanliness and
managed smell, they wear them like armor to protect
themselves from their own insides, they don't want to
look like their own insides, they don't want to bubble
and gurgle and osmotize and squish in squashy blobs of
water bagged in sloppy, sweated skins. Bam! Bam! God
fills the peoples up with frisky goo, love-stuff like snot,
and wraps it up in tissue-paper like a framed photograph
you just had framed at the framing store. "I've been
framed," says the Devil, trapped under glass, missing
his shoes. The Devil pulls his red-haired foot up from
underneath the picture and sticks it through the glass
like a bulbous root or orb that insinuates itself through
a million separate invisible pores in the glass, as if it had
become a root-system of worms, before re-integrating
as a foot in the shape of a hand that shakes the hand of
a murderer who howls in grief because human beings
are unreal flower-pots, not significant enough to feel
meaningful while murdering. And God arrives as an
army-recruiter, and gives the poor murderous boy the
right stuff, the right way to kill, scratches out the word
"murder" with a hundred strokes of a dull pencil until
the paper tears and the face of a dead woman or a dead
child is briefly visible until the paper is sewn up and
nothing can be seen except the words "inevitable price
of war" written by a dead lawyer in the Pentagon whose
soul has been refined into an injectable solution called

"Media Patriotism," a few quick shots of which make people feel they are being patriotic just by shutting the fuck up and allowing the General-Beyond-The-Grave to wear God's shoes. God was wearing the Devil's shoes, and the General-Beyond-The-Grave was wearing God's shoes, and the Devil's bare feet were human hearts. It is an imposter universe, where old con men love to be conned because when they are being taken for a ride they can forget about human duplicity. The General-Beyond-The-Grave, God, and the Devil are the three sides of a Love Triangle that add up to the Con-Man-Over-All. The Devil is the shortest side; his leg of the Triangle is the radius of Earth. The General and God each preside over long legs that reach from the Earth to the center of the Sun. These long legs belong to a blond named Trinity who is drinking a glass of water in her bedroom under the covers while she watches a movie about brave men who are making the world a place where her room can exist and she can exist in it, naked as a saint, and the television can exist and tell stories about the brave men who enable all this to exist: they might be firefighters, astronauts, kayak-enthusiasts, soldiers, police, lawyers. . .advertisers, packagers of stories, theologians, nationalists, poets, salesmen. . .The General-Beyond-The-Grave listens to tape-recordings of war and disciplines them by saying a commanding word in-sync with every scream. Packaged subliminally, screams are inserted into every Amen, between the "A" and "m", adding limitless depth of emotion to the simplest act of agreement with the Good Lord's Policies.

THE END

The End

Time and space, they are too big.
Human beings, they are too varied.
The world has become too complex
and laughs at how ideas are simple.

Ideas want to get back to their place above the world,
rather than being trapped inside of hermeneutic
convolutions that are the long intestine
of time and space, extending reality
into smaller and smaller sub-genres of incident
by diluting ideas so that they fit all moods,
until all people are full to the brim with their own
cocktail of disharmonious contradiction.

Then comes the Judge with his great big Gavel
Beating on Time and Space!
And Time and Space seek shelter
with relatives, or in a halfway house.

Everything falls from the sky: Bombs,
friends, memories, flowers,
doors and windows, the beginnings of conversations,
Testaments, Wills, baby pictures,
Jesus, Moses, the face of Jesus in a Jackson Pollock,
blood that catches fire when exposed to sunlight,
fire that freezes, transfixed by the sight of blood.

Innocent head,
Eternal bed,
Goodnight Time and Space.
Infinite light,
No Eye in sight,
No day nor night, place or face.

Ark

The Ark of National Security loitered on the waters.
Dead animals stunk in the belly of the ship.
Dolphins leapt in the receding waters;
mountains began to show their top-most points.
Noah's shiny uniform, which his wife had sewn,
of cloth of the blue-black color that is the daylight
surrendering and welcoming the night,
color that is the night impregnated with ebbing daylight.
From this color she sewed his uniform,
and the buttons she formed of the sounds
of the whole wealth of a great house being thrown,
dishes crashing, with great force into a sink.
As the flood receded, Noah unbuttoned his coat.
His casual attire, shown in the sunlight, gave pleasure to God.
His casual attire gave comfort to all eyes,
after such strictness had been shown.
Dead animals stunk in the belly of the ship.
Live animals stunk worse, having rolled in dung and rutted.
The Ark of National Security loitered on the waters
and settled on a mountain like a tooth.
Noah's shiny uniform explained Death in the mild sunlight,
which surrendered and mingled with the cloth.
The blue-black color of the uniform exalted Death,
as something through which the chosen may receive advantages,
as the mild sunlight hid its light within the blue-black cloth.
Dolphins touched each other in the fading-away waters.
Live animals declined to wash themselves,
because the waters smelled like death to them.

Once upon a time,
Time came to an end
In the speculating consciousness of Professor.
The sun barked like a dog and balked and barfed
And it was off, leaving only a russet stain faraway from itself
Like an oil-drop diffusing in a pool,
A drop of yellow egg-yolk oil diffusing in a pool of total
        darkness,
Lack of entity, unmatter
In a particleless sizeless unvastness
Outside the sphere of where things are and when they are.

The unmaterial universe,
Which belched forth anomalous matter
Because even non-existent antigods
Are so depressed that they try suicide
By creating universes that abhor and abolish them
Within their very unselved unwhereness.

But the sun is a small smidge,
The whole thing is rotting
To a point that particles just turn their backs and disappear,
And so, inside of beings
There is an increasing lightness.

Just try to be made of atoms if you don't contain any quarks!
Hah! In the mind of Professor,
This dis[ ]xisting is a witticism.
Whaa Hoo-hah! And in the mind of Professor,
Taloned chimps of throneroom
Throw barbed insults of the purest gold,
That stick on the opponent's fur
And are carried everywhere
Like perfect bitter badges.
And in the mind of unmind mindlessness
A non-voice belches backwards

Swallowing its uncreative juices as if some snake shat its

    tongue.

And in time and after time,

Timely surprises attach wings

To the puny little forearms of

The loved babies in sobbed carriages.

And universes resembling

Loving gentle baskets

And a wicker mask behind which

Modesty drips flowers in a teacup.

And babies spray shrill noises into the

Humming surroundings

Which the ear is so eager to tune in.

And tuned-out digital readouts

Fluctuate and record

The noise-to-signal ratio,

As the beholder's eye expands

And swallows the remote control that is.

I.

The reason there are seven days in the week
Is because it takes seven years
To replenish the soil
After some freak pollution-accident contaminates it.

You are supposed to remember the number.
It is also the ideal number of children to have.

Seven years for the soil to rebuild its cleanliness,
After some freak pollution-accident contaminates it.
Seven days in the week like seven everlasting graves
Of seven ideal children, or six, or five,

Into contamination's chariot balloon.
We all must board the
Charity balloon
Into polite oblivion.

II.

All the people ever killed have only been a test.
I will put a barn above your living
To survive the unbelievable war.
It will be a barn with ten-foot think steel walls.

I will put the name "**I AM**" in golden letters
On the barn, and animals of fur and warmth and breath
Will share the barn with you.
The war is the way that you have been thinking.

Tragedies fill the air of the world like an unclean scent.
Industrial byproducts fill the water of the world.
An unclean taint, the aftertaste of water is suspicion.
It will be a humble barn, full of clean air.

III.

An endless number of corridors expand beneath the earth.
These are the corridors where the killers will hide from death.
They will bring death on the earth by saying the wrong words.
They will bring death on the earth by taunting each other,

Taunting each other's red buttons, laughing at each other's
Weak citizens building weak war-machines that fall apart,
Missiles that cannot rise from the launching-site,
Airplanes with wings that fall off and the pilots die,

Tanks in which electrical fires burn the flesh of the men,
Cannons whose snouts detonate and fill the air with
     shrapnel,
Soldiers whose bodies cease to work when accidental steel
Flies through them, soldiers whose bodies cease to work
     when nerves

Tingle on the middle of the chest and on the belly and the face,
This tingle is where the bullet or the accident will hit,
Unless you run, boys, unless you run. Jimmy Carter, even
Jimmy Carter is a murderer. Like every President.

Gerald Ford a murderer. Nixon, Johnson, of course,
     of course.
Kennedy a murderer. Eisenhower, Truman, of course,
     of course.
Accidental mushrooms replace and supplement God's image,
Pustules on the face of the invisible power, scarring unseen
     God.

IV.

God's will gets back into this world
By accident, in the form of accidents.
God's will long ago was rejected from this world.
God's will was motionless. Heaven is anywhere without Progress.

Maybe people die very young in Heaven, maybe
In Heaven if you are 30 you will be a wise, wise ancient one.
Maybe crop-failures produce unavoidable famine in Heaven.
You immediately move on from the Earthly Heaven to the
        next one,

An identical place. In any heaven the dead
Disappear and return in the form of flowers which
Are wrapped around the bodies of the young who
        experience love.
God's will is that you should experience love and then
        disappear and become a plant.

Now, Progress, and the False-God formed and shaped by
        Progress
Dominates. The False-God of Progress has steel skin and is
        streamlined
Like a Super-Sonic Airplane or Bullet, like a character from
A Japanese animated show, and from the Ass of the
        False-God, pollutants

Blast forth and contaminate. Black clouds of super-heated Jet-filth
Blast forth and contaminate. Edible things contain greater
        and greater levels
Of toxic metals and petrochemical by-products.
And God's will gets back into the world

By accident, in the form of malfunctions
That make the False-God's super-heated stomach
Detonate and spew Death-toxins uncontrolled.

V.

When we are dead, it will be quiet.
Then we will be in the calm of Heaven.
Children with unlived lives will walk for the first time
A few steps, with the assistance of a father's hands.

They will never see the movie "Star Wars."
They will never see the movie "Indiana Jones."
They won't wait in line to be contaminated.
Did you think that was all that life was?

Sometimes it seems like that is all that life is.
Waiting for explosions to improve the movie.
Contaminated by the desire for action, children
Want to fight the war, they want to fire rays

Of cleansing light from a plastic pistol.
They watch the movie "Star Wars" in their hearts.
Giant charismas inside them teach them loyalty,
They run alongside their friends in joyous imitation of war.

They won't eat artificially-colored
Machine-molded sugar servings,
That make them yell as if their home was worth nothing,
And then sulk in a confused vacant mood in the room
    they call their "Secret Headquarters."

VI.

Secrets from God are OK. You have
Complained and I have listened. You can keep
The war, keep it in your brain like
A candle, it will allow you to look at others

Fearlessly. Fantasies of hurting others will give you
A way to look into their faces without seeming scared.
Of course, you won't really do it,
Not until the war comes along.

The war is the way you have been thinking.
Maybe those who suffer violence will benefit from it.
It's a true tragedy when repetition won't heal anything,
When hitting them again won't make them like it.

VII.

God is a poultice, God is healing aloe.
God is a secret of healed air.
God is walking in the shoes of sick and hungry babies,
In their grown-up shoes, which they will never wear.

God is clean air, in a humble heaven.
God is an earth without missile guidance systems.
God is a conquered war, God is
A vision of the instruments of war torn open and their

Wires and computer-chips and egos full of bubbles of
Humiliated blood
Pulled out and spread out in unplugged piles across
        some field
Where men jump up and down on them with boots on,

God is a scent you cannot stop smelling,
Clean air invades the unhealed tragedy
Which is the way I am thinking.
Everybody ever killed has only been a test,

An emergency alert that wakes the soul
And the soul wakes the body
And the body wakes the mind
And the mind contaminates oblivion with war and pain.

An eagle's defilement pleasing images lived
because they slaughtered spent lies radiant
away omnipotence exclusionary fruit AND coin
acting voice faces roar glued up

Ezek'el saw the wheel
Way up in the middle of the air
A wheel inside a wheel
Way up in the middle of the air

Just let me tell you what a hypocrite'll do
Way up in the middle of the air
city-dwellers watch cooking class smiles pleasure
sexual spin grafting swords for right

They'll talk about me and they'll talk about you
Way up in the middle of the air
People mathematical prophylactics babies wept reasons
yet partake probably half mirrors second

Big wheel moved by faith
Little wheel moved by the grace of God
Ezek'el saw the wheel
Way up in the middle of the air

self-serving found everything seeing wiped moods
heads have wanted bound word throngs
bag all there whose the replication
us will did His moral male

magazine punishing propagate whimpering
microscopes toilet
Just you watch how you walk on that cross
Way up in the middle of the air
face face face like work wanted

from they that they they tape
You miss your step and your soul get lost
Way up in the middle of the air
divine immense rude seriousness decided hope

Ezek'el saw the highbrow
Loosely up in the middle of the air
Big lion's moved by faith
Little wheel moved by the grace of looked

A wheel inside a God's
Way up in the AND of the air
A man's inside a changed
Accepted up in the healed of the air

OF SIN

I prefer to love the sin and hate the sinner. Sins are
delicious; the main problem with them is that they are
performed by such scummy, muddled people. I should
perform the sins; I deserve it. After all, if it weren't for
the individual minds and hearts and identities of humans,
no one would really get hurt by any action, no mat-
ter how vile. The great sinners live in a world of fleshy
automatons motivated by culture; wishing to change
culture, they begin to perform surgery on the "people"
around them.

George Bush's sins are terrific; killing people so
their country can be free, and what free means is that
anything of value can be freely purchased, owned, and
disposed of by Americans in a lawful manner however
they see fit. It's dastardly; I love it. But all his talk about
Christ and human rights ruins it for me. In general, the
beautiful land-grabs of colonialism have been spoiled rot-
ten by the hypocritical soft lies of the invaders, describ-
ing the rapes and the beatings as the physical means
through which angels enter into heathen souls. Angelic
American dollars flow into the heathen Iraqi economy,
transforming it into a futuristic Paradise where white
people far away enrich themselves without ever seeing
the place or raising a hand.

Homicide is a sin beloved by conservatives, because
they know that human beings need to get active doing
God's will and destroying the enemy. God is not going
to act for us; God's will only comes to pass on Earth
if we get out there and bring it to fruition. That's why
God invented free will; we have the opportunity to go
out and do his work or not. As the Reverend Martin

Luther King, Jr. said, "I am coming to feel that the people of ill will have used time much more effectively than the people of good will." The world is back-sliding away from God's plan, and so it's time to grab a gun or knife and get going with some serious homicide. No more tyranny; any people who allow themselves to be tyrannized will have to be methodically slaughtered until they get some backbone. That's why we had to kill the native people: because they had to toughen up and we represented God's scourge on them to punish them for being weak.

People don't like to admit how ruthless God is; they like to think that all the violence and abuse that accompanies His plans is the result of human error. No, my brethren, those crimes were not isolated incidents committed by God's representatives in a lax moment due to error in judgment. The errors in judgment all involve being too nice to the conquered people, because discipline requires severity, and severity requires arbitrary and brutal expressions of power that turn individuals into examples. An individual is not very relevant, but an example defines a higher standard. Tortured Iraqis should be glad for the privilege of being turned into demonstrations of the real (admittedly kinky) nature of God's love.

My definition of sin is anything that goes against God's will. God being a strong cowboy with a rigid code of conduct, sins generally involve being nice to the wrong people. Jesus was a great sinner, of course, and put to death for that reason; that is when liberalism entered heaven. It is Jesus who argues that it is necessary to express kindness for social inferiors while you abuse them. Jesus is God's hypocrisy, by which even He is made an imperfect sinner. Up until then, blood on God's hands couldn't stick. There were no crimes; anyone could do anything they were strong enough to do, as long as they yelled "In the name of the Father" while they did it. Now, God's embarrassed, and passes off all responsibility onto subordinates, none of whom he ever met or had any interaction with before. Do you think God's going to take responsibility for George W. Bush? Please! So George is stuck doing God's will and becoming a sinner because of it. All because of Jesus, there's just no accountability anymore.

God is good; He created spaghetti.

There is a place of steady and consistent indoor lighting
calibrated to appease and clarify the sight.

There is a place of steady, justified anger.

God is God; He created society.
There is arguably something good about it.
I like how it means so much more than you know.

A Bible made of landmines; you read it with your feet.

The world is a 5-paragraph essay written by Satan,
without the use of topic sentences, and with no thesis.
This 5-paragraph essay is entirely plagiarized of God.
But when it is rewritten, the intention changes.

Writing is a process, and therefore false.
Writing embodies as its main aspect DELAY.
Writing slows the writer; reading slows the reader.
God is instantaneous, simultaneous, an insight.

The victims have to reinvent God in their own image again.
All it takes is the ability to look at themselves.
It can take years.
God is waiting in their scary mirrors. God is afraid of them.

A phony Bible is the greatest thing a man can offer to the
        world.

Writing is to plot, to scheme, to propagandize.
God calls on propagandists to attack fake Gods,
it's wearying, all the writing, petty pot-shots, pokes.

There is a place of sadness where Jesus likes to go

on his bad days and cuddle the dead bodies.
Their spirits are playing in a higher world,
playing tag, long-jumping between fluffy flying clouds.

But some days Jesus likes to lay down with the bodies,
in a vast mass-grave at the center of God's thoughts.

From there, the spirits are invisible.

𝅘𝅥

LES FIGUES PRESS
Post Office Box 7736
Los Angeles, CA 90007
www.lesfigues.com